Artistic Visions

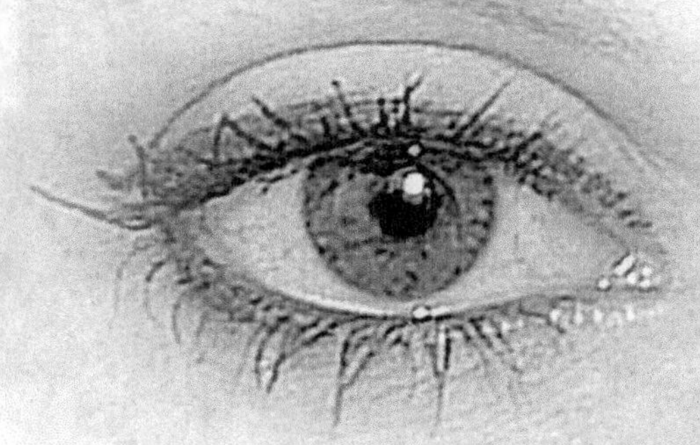

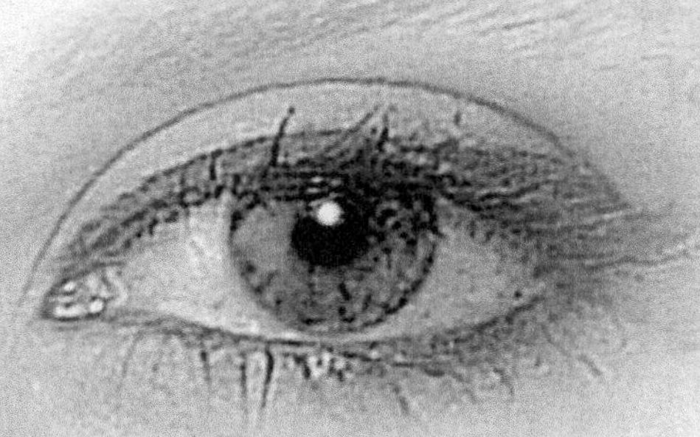

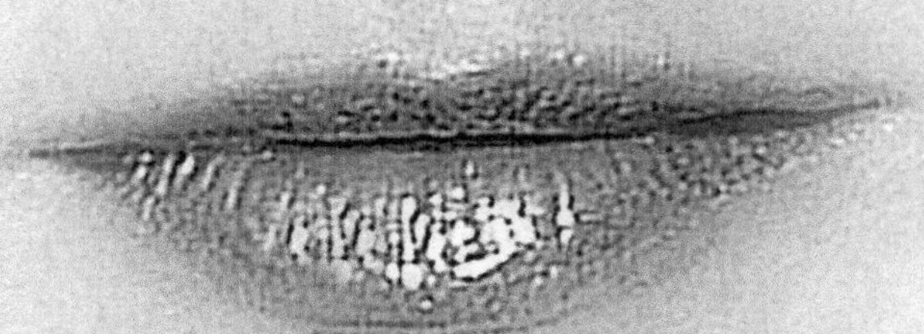

Hairstylists' step-by-step guide to getting published

by

Vittoria Natale

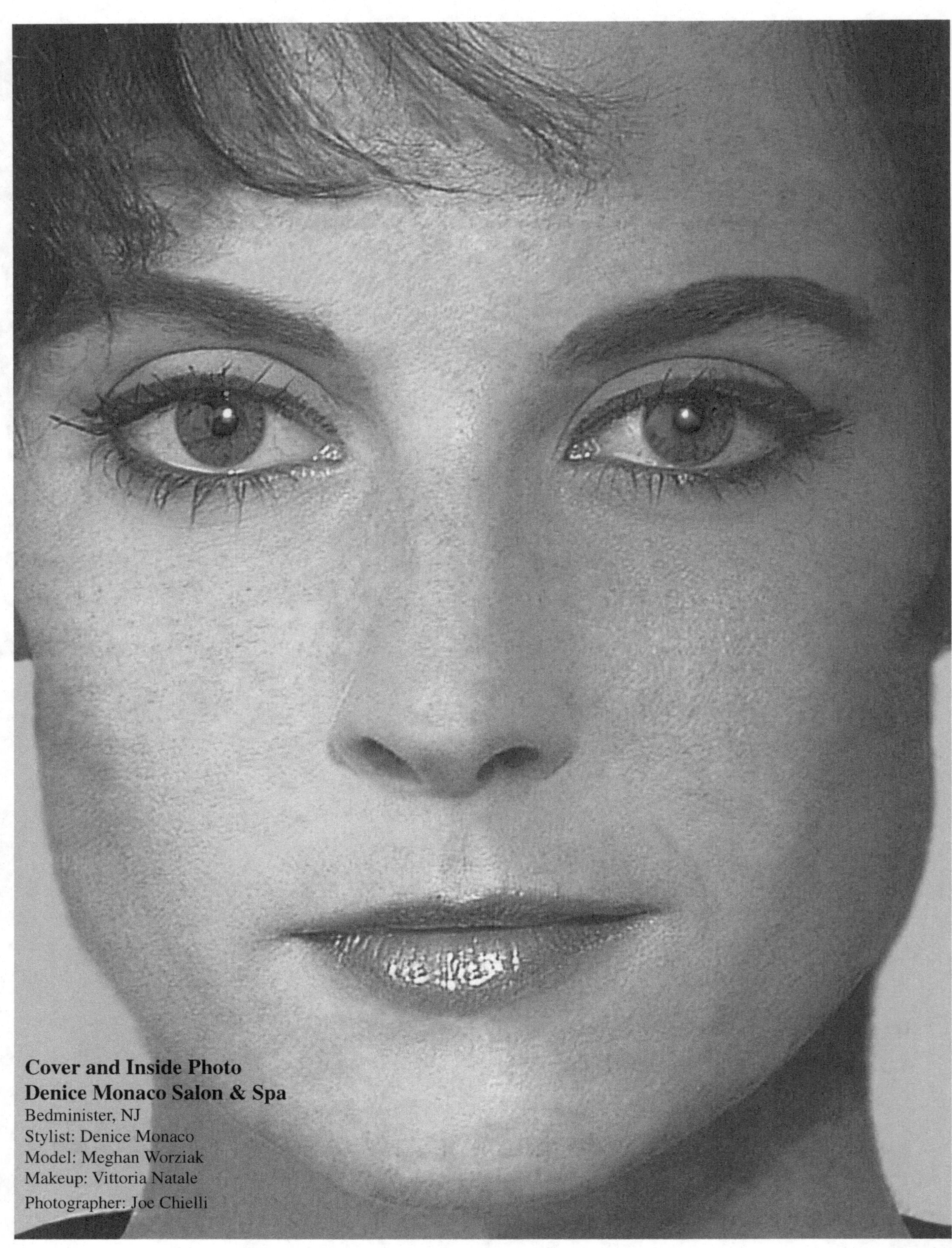

Cover and Inside Photo
Denice Monaco Salon & Spa
Bedminister, NJ
Stylist: Denice Monaco
Model: Meghan Worziak
Makeup: Vittoria Natale
Photographer: Joe Chielli

Order this book online at www.trafford.com
or email orders@trafford.com

Most Trafford titles are also available at major online book retailers.

Print information available on the last page.

ISBN: 978-1-4120-1415-1 (sc)
ISBN: 978-1-4907-8177-8 (e)

Trafford rev. 03/31/2017

www.trafford.com
North America & international
toll-free: 1 888 232 4444 (USA & Canada)
fax: 812 355 4082

Artistic Visions

Hairstylists' Step-by-Step Guide to Getting Published

Author

Vittoria Natale

Editors

Gilda Morigi & Martha Ledger

Featured Photographers

Joe Chielli, Church Street Studios; Joe Edelman, Joe Edelman PhotographicS; Gary Mattie, Mattie Studio; Paul Rumohr, Paul Rumohr Photography; Tom Carson, Tom Carson Photography; Jonathan Martin, Jonathan Martin Photography

Hairstylists

Christina McClure, Salon Gallimore; Denice Monaco Salon & Spa; Isabel Rivera, Freelance Hairstylist; Regina Webb, Regina Webb Salon & Spa; Stephanie Lawson, Erica Lino and Rachel Tibbetts, Hot Locks SalonSpa; Sarah Mize, Beej Haircolor Studio; Genoveva Rodriguez, Collections Salons & Day Spas; Jennifer Dorsey, Over the Rainbow Salon & Spa

Models

Alison, Amanda, BriAnna Casantini, Dawne, Deidre, Gina, Hilary, Irina Soriano, Jaclyn, Jade, Julia Elkouss, Kara, Kiara, Madeline, Melissa and Terry and Maria Gingrich and Megan Wozniak of the Bowman Agency

Graphic Design

James Chielli, Church Street Studios

All makeup by Vittoria Natale

ARTISTIC VISION

ARTISTIC/ar-tis-tic/adj
1:showing imaginative skill in arrangement or execution (artistic photography)
Merriam-Webster Dictionary

VISION/ vizh-en/n
1:something seen otherwise than by ordinary sight (as in a dream or trance) 2:a vivid picture created by the imagination 3:the act or power of imagination 4:the act or power of seeing
The American Heritage Dictionary of the English Language

"We see with our eyes, but true vision comes from the mind."
Vittoria Natale

This book is for everyone who has the vision to pursue his or her dreams.

contents

INTRODUCTION

First let me say that Artistic Vision comes from the mind. What you can imagine, you can create.

There are no rules governing images. But, once you have a specific idea about the color, length and design of the models' hair, the easier it will be to produce strong, defined, marketable images.

If your goal is to build a salon image, and plan to decorate it solely with pictures, and if you wish to increase publicity for the salon, then this guide is a great place to get started.

For many hairstylists, the desire to be published begins with a commitment, of time, money and effort. But it's a commitment that will bring many rewards: both in personal satisfaction and financial success. As soon as you've succeeded in publishing your first piece, you will have embarked on an ongoing campaign that will allow you to share your styles with the world.

As you become more involved with styling hair for the camera, you will be amazed at how versatile and creative you will become. You will begin to envision your own unique designs captured on film. Your vision will supply the magic to create great looks and the only boundary will be the limits of your imagination.

The guidelines, tips, forms, and suggestions in this manual are the result of both research and observation. They were compiled from the most reliable sources in the beauty industry, including published stylists, makeup artists, fashion photographers, magazine editors, and art directors. I gathered their advice, and consulted with others in the field, to produce the information provided in the manual.

STAGES OF PLANNING

THE GRAND PLAN

Planning is everything. You can make adjustments—hopefully inspired ones—at the time of the photo shoot, but all major decisions must be made well in advance.

First, you must choose the look you want to achieve. It could be high fashion, retro, classic, avant-garde or theme-driven, such as an updated 40s look, where the model has long, layered, wavy dark hair, manicured eyebrows, long lashes, rosy cheeks, full soft red lips and is, wearing a fitted suit jacket accessorized with gloves and a choker.

Next, you must determine how you'll produce the desired look. What type of cut is required? Will coloring the hair reinforce what you're after? Will you need special hair products? If, for example, you're doing a 40s style that recalls starlets like Rita Hayworth and Veronica Lake, your plan might be the following: Using a model with slightly longer than shoulder-length hair, do an elongated-U cut which falls just below the shoulder area and then work it with setting lotion or light-hold gel to create waves, a light-hold hairspray to curl the hair with a curling iron, and a medium-hold hairspray applied as a finishing step.

Do you want black-and-white images or color ones? Black-and-white might be appropriate for a retro look. Color would be better for a high-fashion image. The photographer, makeup artist, and fashion stylist will all need your decision in advance of the shoot. Keep in mind, too, the magazines you'd like your photographs to appear in. Do they use mostly color or mostly black-and white.

Decide what clothes and jewelry are best suited to complete the total look. If you're after a retro effect, pearls or a choker would be appropriate. Visible tattoos and multiple ear piercings, on the other hand, would support a style that's avant-garde.

Makeup can range from totally natural to hyper-dramatic. You need to identify what along this spectrum matches the look you're seeking and then be able to explain your creative choice to the makeup artist.

And finally, before you start to assemble your team, decide

who's going to direct the shoot—you or the photographer. If you're dealing with relative newcomers to keep costs down, you may have to supervise them all. If, however, the photographer and makeup artist are experienced professionals, they'll know how to achieve your vision with a minimum of verbal direction. The clearer you are about what you want, the easier it will be for them to work creatively. Try collecting photographs and build a picture book that best represents the looks you're after. The discipline will lead to greater clarity on your part.

Once you've chosen the look and the means to achieve it, you're ready for action. Here's a step-by-step plan.

1. Select your team: a photographer, makeup artist, and someone to assist you. Describe the nature of the shoot to them. Explain the kind of images you're seeking.

2. Set a photo shoot date and confirm it with all members of the team.

3. Select the most attractive models that you can find. Have the photographer approve your choices.

4. Arrange a pre-cut or color date, approximately three or four days prior to the shoot.

5. Select clothing and jewelry or hire a fashion stylist for the photo session.

6. Target publications that publish the kind of styles you are creating. If you are doing short and sexy styles, the newsstand magazine *Short & Sexy Hairstyles* should be on your list. If you're doing shoulder-length Rita Hayworth look-a-likes, don't bother sending *Short & Sexy Hairstyles* your photos. They're not going to be interested, no matter how good your work is.

7. Hold the photo session.

8. Sort and select images. Refer to the target publications.

9. Edit photos with the photographer. Request cropping (reframing the image) where necessary or an adjustment of values or colors?

10. Send selected photos to publications, keeping their deadline in mind.

11. Keep track of responses. Analyze what images get accepted or rejected.

12. Send thank-you notes to magazine editors or art directors.

Notes

THE TEAM

The team that will be selected will determine the outcome of the session. Selections can be made through advertisements and suitable contacts you may have already made. Look for people who understand what you want to achieve. Professional photo sessions are costly and are successful only if they are properly coordinated. Like any other business plan, a good strategy is essential. Be prepared to pay for the best. If you cannot afford top talent immediately, save your money and schedule photo shoots fewer times a year. It is better to spend $2,000 to $3,000 twice a year and get good results than $500 four times a year and get poor ones.

The Photographer

Excellent photography can have a powerful impact and convey a clear message about you and the image you want to portray to the public. A good photo session will depend on the quality and creativity of the photographer you select.

An excellent photographer will both enhance and capture the look you are creating. Some excellent photographers will be able to do it better than other excellent photographers because they've made this type of shooting their specialty. The American Society of Media Photographers (ASMP) lists 62 photographic categories. These include niches such as corporate, landscapes, interiors, events, photojournalism, etc. The specialties that will serve you are fashion, beauty, and glamour. You definitely don't want a portrait photographer. A portrait doesn't make a fashion statement.

ASMP has 40 chapters throughout the U.S., and their web site (www.asmp.org) is one place you might start your search for a local photographer who specializes in photographing hair. You can also contact local modeling agencies for names of photographers that hire models for your kind of shoot. Or you can cruise the Yellow Pages. Some photographers list their specialties.

Never hire a photographer without a portfolio check, even if he or she comes highly recommended. Ask to see many images, not just one or two. Does his or her style appeal to you? Is the work sufficiently professional to appear in commercial magazines? Has the photographer been published in any national or international magazines?

Visit the photographer's studio. You'll be able to see the equipment available and judge his or her potential to do exciting things with lighting and sets. The studio should also have a private dressing area for the model and appropriate work space that includes mirrors, lights, and counters for the makeup artist.

Assess the photographer's personality. You want someone who is decisive and confident, not someone who is so egotistical that he or she won't listen to your ideas and concerns. Fortunately, most photographers will be very accommodating because they want future work from you.

A good photographer will shoot Polaroids as his or her own check before putting the image on film and will review the Polaroids with you. If the shoot is done digitally, both you and the photographer will be able to see how the image looks on the camera's screen or on a computer screen while the shoot is still in progress. Each of you can make adjustments in lighting or makeup if you spot problems. These days, nobody need be surprised by final prints that miss the mark. To benefit from this technology, you must be an active observer during the shoot. Don't go out for lunch unless the photographer does.

When you find a photographer you're comfortable with, ask for prices. The day-rate for a studio shoot by an experienced photographer can be $1,000 to $3,000+ a day. This should cover the film, processing, contact sheets, prints, assistants' fees, and equipment rental. Beware of prices that are considerably lower. Ask if everything is included? Ask if there are other potential charges? If the photographer is working digitally, ask what the cost is for having the images downloaded onto a CD? This is a way to view them on your computer. Negotiate for total buyout rights so you own the film. Get all quotes in writing. Have the photographer list everything that is included. A deposit is usually required to secure a date.

The Professional Makeup Artist

A studio photographer employs a whole spectrum of lighting techniques. She or he can bathe a subject in everything from a warm, mellow light to one that's blue-tinged and icy-crisp. She or he can also use colored gels over the lights and increase the palette. A photographic makeup artist understands lighting techniques, too, and how to coordinate makeup with whatever lighting is selected. Photographic makeup is more than just colors painted on a face. It is the combination of imagination and carefully practiced technique. If the makeup application is good and the photographer's lighting is good, all colors will be rendered correctly in the photographs.

The photographic makeup specialist is also trained to convert imperfect features into ones that look perfect. In real life we are constantly in motion, and many facial imperfections escape our notice. Not so in a photograph. Here the image is frozen and can be carefully studied. A good makeup artist will achieve eyes that appear identical in shape, because if one seems larger than the other—and most people's eyes are not a matched pair—it will make the face look crooked and the smaller eye will appear droopy. The makeup artist will also create perfectly symmetrical lips.

In the final image, the colors will appear well-blended. There won't be any sharp demarcation lines, unless these are part of a special-effects design that was determined in advance. But even in the most severe, avant-garde styles, the makeup should never appear gaudy or garish.

Finding a skilled makeup artist is not easy. Unlike photographers, they don't have a professional organization, and they also don't self-advertise in great numbers in the Yellow Pages. However, the photographer you've selected will have worked with makeup artists, and can probably recommend one with whom she or he already has a good rapport. Modeling agencies may also maintain a list of local makeup artists they like. Check this out. Call some agencies. Maybe they represent makeup artists as well as models. It's a great way to find both makeup artists and models at the same time. If they do, schedule an appointment to meet with the booker at the agency to review the makeup artists' work.

But before you take the photographer's or agency's word about a makeup artist, you need to do the same kind of portfolio check you did with the photographer. Ask questions. Has the person's work been published? How often? In what kind of magazines? Does the person do different looks for color and black-and-white?

What does the person charge? The range for photo makeup work is $350 to $600+ a day depending on the market. If you can't find a photo makeup specialist or can't afford a pro, give your salon makeup artist a try. But arrange a test shoot first. Use one model and one hairstyle. Discuss the look you want to achieve. Show the salon artist pictures you've clipped from magazines that have a similar look. Share your observations while the makeup is being applied. Review the final photos together to see what worked and what didn't. This represents an exciting opportunity for the salon artist so he or she is sure to put out extra effort.

The Styling Assistant

Just as you require assistants in your hair salon to shampoo clients, wrap perms, prepare equipment and straighten up, you'll need an assistant for the photo shoot. This person will free you from small tasks and let you concentrate on the job of styling.

An assistant is not a lackey. Choose a person whose ability you respect and someone you work well with. Choose someone who also respects you. The level of professional expertise you need from the assistant will depend on you. As the stylist you must make that decision.

Decide in advance what tasks the assistant will do prior to and during the photo session. Your list might include helping out during the pre-color and pre-cut in the salon; preparing a schedule for the models; setting up blow dryers, curling irons and hair-care products at the studio; and shampooing models on the day of the shoot. Make up a schedule for the assistant that establishes the order of tasks. Review the schedule together before the day of the shoot.

Studio
Stylist: Christina McClure
Model: BriAnna Casantini
Makeup: Vittoria Natale
Photographer: Gary Mattie

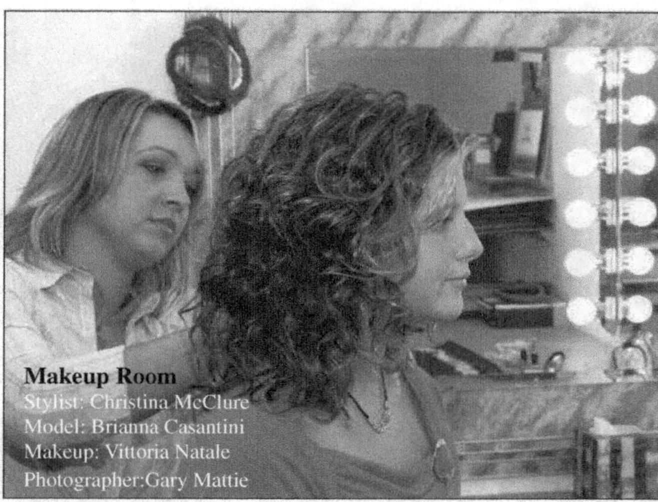

Makeup Room
Stylist: Christina McClure
Model: Brianna Casantini
Makeup: Vittoria Natale
Photographer:Gary Mattie

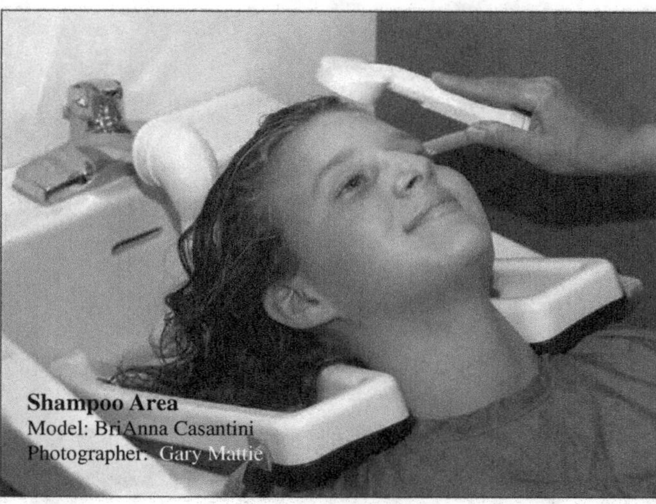

Shampoo Area
Model: BriAnna Casantini
Photographer: Gary Mattie

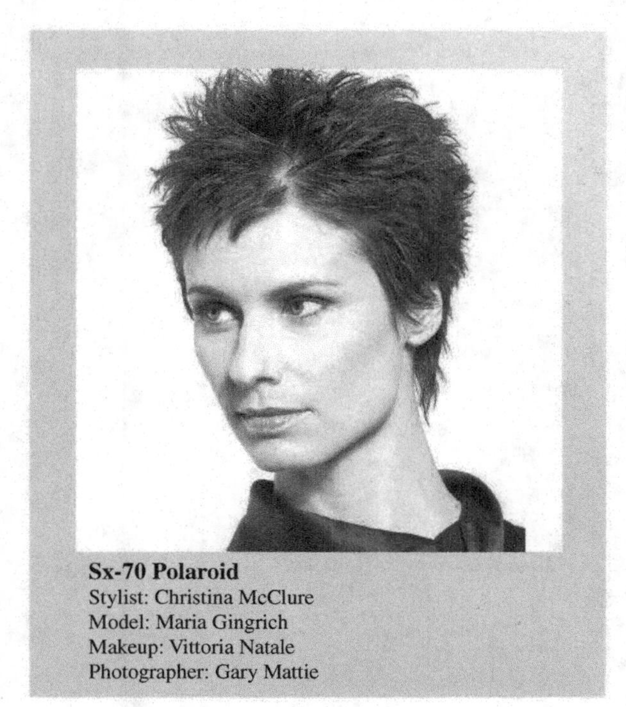

Sx-70 Polaroid
Stylist: Christina McClure
Model: Maria Gingrich
Makeup: Vittoria Natale
Photographer: Gary Mattie

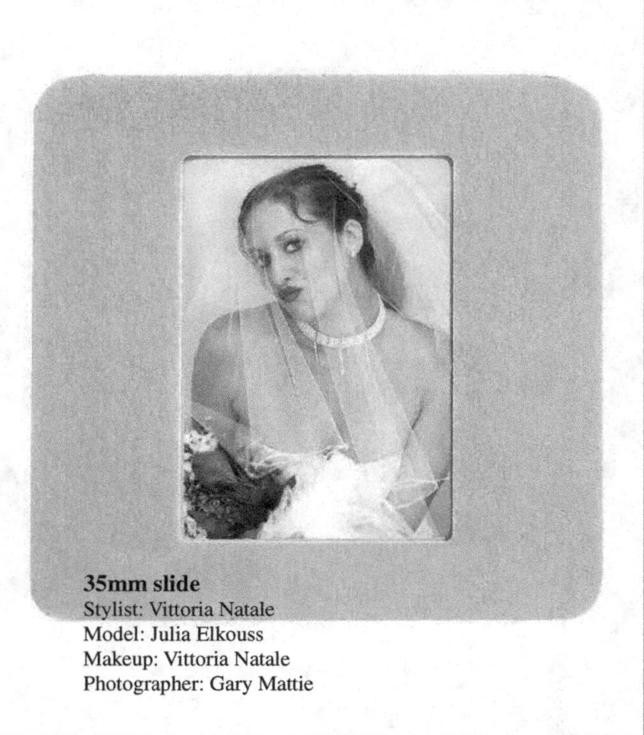

35mm slide
Stylist: Vittoria Natale
Model: Julia Elkouss
Makeup: Vittoria Natale
Photographer: Gary Mattie

Notes

DATES & DEADLINES

Choosing a Photo Session Date

Choosing a date may sound as simple as looking at a calendar and saying, this day looks good. But in truth, there are some tricky calculations you must make.

Magazine content is always coordinated with a season (fall, winter, spring, summer) and is selected three or four months in advance of an issue's publication date. Ask the magazine you've targeted for its publication calendar. Or check an issue. Most publications that accept submissions have their deadlines listed in the back of the book. Choose a future-issue deadline and count backwards three or four months.

Magazine deadlines are real. The staff needs time to write, edit and proof material; the art department must design each page; the production team has to prepare everything for the printer. Advertisers want the publication in circulation when promised. If it's late, they don't pay for their ads.

If you miss a seasonal deadline, you're out of luck. Editors know what they need and what they can't use. Calling and making a pest of yourself will make your work unwelcome in the future.

The aftermath of a photo shoot must also be figured into your date-selection calculations. Film must be processed and contact sheets printed. Choosing images, editing them, reviewing and mailing prints can easily take two or three weeks. Add this time to the three or four months the magazine needs.

This means, if you want to publish a winter collection of styles in a December issue (publication date: November 18), you should schedule your photo shoot, at the latest, for the end of June. If you've targeted foreign magazines, make it a week or two earlier to allow for increased travel time and customs clearance.

The date selected should be convenient for everyone involved. Stay clear of major holidays or even holiday weekends. No one likes to give up these special days. Non-holiday weekends and Mondays are good times. Many salons are closed on Mondays and business is generally light in those that are open.

When you've found a date that's agreeable to everybody, make it firm with a deposit to both the photographer and makeup artist. Otherwise, someone else may offer money up-front and your team may decide to take it. Of course, a deposit means that if you have to cancel, you're going to be out a chunk of money. But this is only fair because your team may have turned down other work for that day based on a commitment they made to you.

If the photographer or makeup artist cancels, you should get your full deposit back at the time of cancellation. Both should sign for deposits they receive and agree in writing about refunding it. They should also understand that cancelling because a higher-paying job comes along is unacceptable.

If either the photographer or makeup artist cancels, you're entitled to an explanation. You may not believe the reason given. If you don't, say so, but don't argue. Just make a note to yourself not to use this person in the future.

Notes

Hot Locks SalonSpa
Passion Partners: North Falmouth, MA
Stylist: Rachel Tibbets
Colorist: Rachel Tibbets
Model: Alison
Makeup: Vittoria Natale
Photographer: Tom Carson

Regina Webb Salon & Spa
Passion Partners: Bowling Green, KY
Stylist: Regina Webb
Model: Dawne
Makeup: Vittoria Natale
Photographer: Tom Carson

Hot Locks SalonSpa
Passion Partners: North Falmouth, MA
Stylist: Stephanie Lawson
Colorist: Stephanie Lawson
Model: Kiara
Makeup: Vittoria Natale
Photographer: Tom Carson

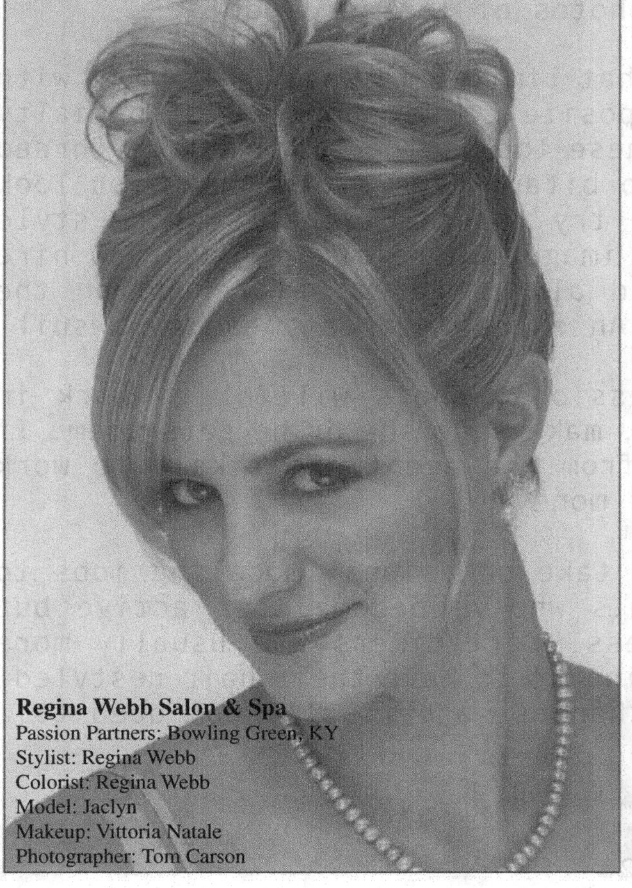

Regina Webb Salon & Spa
Passion Partners: Bowling Green, KY
Stylist: Regina Webb
Colorist: Regina Webb
Model: Jaclyn
Makeup: Vittoria Natale
Photographer: Tom Carson

Regina Webb Salon & Spa
Passion Partners: Bowling Green, KY
Stylist: Regina Webb
Colorist: Regina Webb
Model: Terry
Makeup: Vittoria Natale
Photographer: Tom Carson

MODELS

Selecting the models

Any honest editor will tell you that a great cut on a mediocre face will have less chance of being published than a mediocre cut on a great face. One well-known and incredibly great-looking model has appeared in more than 20 publications in just one hairstyle. One publication ran every angle of the cut. The success the stylist enjoyed had a lot to do with the model's superb face.

Such faces are rare, but this doesn't mean that you shouldn't try to find one. There are lots of potential models around—everyone from your really cute next-door neighbor to an agency professional. Your approach will differ depending on the type of model you deal with.

A professional model will be under contract to a modeling agency, which means a percentage of the fee the model earns goes to the agency. Usually, you pay the agency directly. It takes its cut and then pays the model. If you've never worked before with the agency you contact, you'll need to visit and explain what you're looking for. If you've already published hairstyles, take tear sheets with you to show the quality of your work. The agency will let you review the composite cards and photos of lots of models.

Interestingly, you're somewhat limited in what you can do with a professional model. Their composite cards show their specialty looks. If you radically change these looks, the model may be forced to redo the card. The cost is exorbitant. Therefore, when you look at the agency's composite cards, try to select models whose style and hair length are close to the image you're after. When you hire a professional model, you should always agree beforehand on the amount of hair that can be cut. An extra inch can mean a lawsuit.

If you come across a professional who's willing to work in exchange for photographic prints, make sure she or he gets them. If she or he doesn't, no one else from the agency is likely to work with you in the future, even for money.

Part-time models are people who take occasional modeling jobs to make extra money or professionals who've become less active but still keep a hand in the business. Part-timers are usually more agreeable than full-time professionals to have their hair restyled. Even they, while allowing some changes, are usually not open to a radical makeover. Smaller agencies have more part-timers than large agencies. Agencies connected to a modeling school can also usually provide a good selection of part-timers. The modeling students they represent are one of your best options. They have the most to gain by participating in a hair photo-shoot. They need experience and contact with people who use models. Not having worked professionally yet, they have no tear sheets and few, if any, professional-quality photos of themselves. Your photo session is an opportunity to get both. And they may also need to have their look updated and welcome some radical hairstyling.

Then there are amateurs. These are people who never thought about modeling. They are your attractive clients, friends, friends of friends and even people you may notice on the street. Signing them on may require a lot of persuasion, and they may be nervous at first when in front of the camera. But after a few shoots, they just might turn into excellent models for you.

When you approach amateurs, give them your business card and explain what you'd like to do. Arrange an appointment for them at your salon, so they know you're a serious stylist and reputable business person. Describe what you'd like to do to their hair. If they agree to a tryout, cut less, never more, than you say you will. If they work out well, offer to take care of their hair free for a year. Remember, a great face is hard to find.

Before you run off in search of the face that magazines will love to publish, keep in mind that while everyone has different concepts of beauty, the camera has a fairly narrow definition.

What photographs best is a model with a good jaw line; stay away from weak or pointy chins. The camera also likes full lips, rather than thin ones, which tend to appear pursed or angry. The upper should be slightly larger than the lower. The nose is the facial feature that is closest to the camera, and the camera will tend to exaggerate its problems. Choose a nose that has a refined bridge and a straight rather than a turned-up tip. The nostrils should not be too wide. The camera also loves big almond-shaped eyes. So does the makeup artist because large lids always seem ample enough for the application of color. Small, squinty eyes are less photogenic, but makeup can often make them look significantly larger. Brows can be dark or light, but a very high arch will give the model a startled look.

A good attitude is almost as important as looks. The model

must enjoy being in front of the camera and the center of attention. You're also looking for someone who is confident enough in his or her own looks to be comfortable with a changed appearance. You don't want a model who'll tell you how he or she wants to look in the photo. They're on the wrong track when they think the photo is about them.

Notes

10875 Main Street ~ Suite 205 ▪ Fairfax, VA 22030 USA ▪ 703-359-6000
www.MktgSols.com ▪ MktgSols@MktgSols.com ▪ Fax: 703-934-5490

PASSION STYLEBOOK
~ MODEL INTERVIEW & APPLICATION SHEET ~

PLEASE ATTACH CURRENT PHOTOGRAPH!

All Haircutting, Haircolor and Hairstyling Services will be provided on a complimentary basis.
Your Model Application will be considered for Passion Stylebooks and any of our Marketing Solutions client's photography sessions.
Most photography sessions will require you to allow us to create a new haircut, haircolor and hairstyle for you.
We are always interested in hair, skin, nail and spa models!

Name: ______________________ Home Phone: ______________________
Cellular Phone: __________ Work Phone: __________ Email Address: __________
Address: ______________________ City, State & Zip: ______________________
Age: _____ Date of Birth: __ / __ / ____ Height: ______ Weight: ____ Measurements: __________
Sizes: Shirt: ______ Skirt: ______ Pants: ______ Shoes: ____ Other: _________: __________

CURRENT HAIRCUT & HAIRSTYLE:
Hair Length: ☐ Short ☐ Medium ☐ Long Describe: ______________________
Natural Haircolor: ☐ Blonde ☐ Brunette ☐ Redhead ☐ ______________________
Recent Haircolor Services: ______________________ When: __________
Recent Perm / Relaxer Services: ______________________ When: __________
Hair Texture: ☐ Straight ☐ Wavy ☐ Curly ☐ ______________________
Hair Density: ☐ Fine ☐ Medium ☐ Thick ☐ ______________________
Regular Hairstylist: ______________________ My Current Salon: ______________________

OPTIONS & LIMITS ON HAIR MAKEOVER:
☐ **YES, I AM OPEN TO ALL SUGGESTIONS** with ***"NO LIMITS!"***
______ My Haircut & Length Guidelines: ______________________
______ My Haircolor & Highlighting Guidelines: ______________________
______ My Perm & Relaxer Guidelines: ______________________
______ 'Makeover Suggestions' For Yourself: ______________________

SKIN QUALITY & COLOR:
Eyes - Color & Shape: ☐ Blue ☐ Brown ☐ Grey ☐ Hazel ☐ __________
Straight Teeth & Smile: ☐ Fair ☐ Good ☐ Great ☐ __________
Any Distinguishing Features, Scars or Tattoos: ☐ Yes ☐ No ☐ __________
Any Allergies or Nervous Reactions: ☐ Yes ☐ No ☐ __________
Any Required Waxing & Hair Removal Services: ☐ Yes ☐ No ☐ __________
HANDS - NAIL & SKIN QUALITY: ☐ Fair ☐ Good ☐ Great ☐ __________
FEET & LEGS - NAIL & SKIN QUALITY: ☐ Fair ☐ Good ☐ Great ☐ __________
BACK & CHEST - SKIN & BODY: ☐ Fair ☐ Good ☐ Great ☐ __________
COMFORTABLE WITH SPA & BODY PHOTOGRAPHY: ☐ Yes ☐ No ☐ __________

PREVIOUS MODELING EXPERIENCES: ______________________

INTERVIEW NOTES: ______________________

☐ Confirmed ☐ Not Confirmed ☐ Next Time ☐ Date & Call Time: ______ __________

QUESTIONS? Call Larry Oskin at Marketing Solutions ~ 703-359-6000

Notes

Notes

FASHION

The camera records whatever you put in front of it, and what the model is wearing contributes to the overall look you're trying to achieve as much as the hairstyle and makeup. Clothing and accessories should enhance the image, not dominate it. Pair an easy summer cut with casual clothing, a glamorous hairstyle with something dressy. Curb the tendency to overdo it. It's best to keep the outfit simple and stay focused on the hair.

The easiest way to ensure a consistent look is to hire a fashion stylist. Once you carefully explain the image you're after, the stylist will pull together clothing, jewelry, a hair ornament perhaps and other props that reinforce your style statement.

Modeling agencies and fashion photographers will be able to recommend fashion stylists they've worked with. You can expect to pay anywhere from $300 to $500+ for a day-long photo shoot. Or since all fashion professionals need to keep their portfolios updated, you might get lucky and find someone who'll work in exchange for prints.

If your budget doesn't allow you to hire a fashion stylist, you can, of course, be your own fashion stylist. But beware, this is time-consuming work. First, you have to scout out who sells what you need. The total look may be split among several stores: a sequined evening dress here; pearl ropes there; a fur piece a little further down the road. And once you find the fashions, you have to get permission to borrow them. This may entail another visit to meet with the store owner or phone calls or a letter. You must pick up everything right before the shoot and return it as soon as the shoot ends so that the merchandise is quickly available again for purchase. And finally, you need to do something nice for the merchant who lends you his goods.(The store owner might welcome prints from the shoot to advertise the store. Ask the photographer to provide an extra set. But be clear about whom they're for. If the photographer doesn't give permission, he or she can demand compensation later on for the unauthorized commercial use of his or her work. The photographer may ask a higher fee anyway, if knowing that the prints will have multiple uses.)

With all this potential work, doesn't hiring a fashion stylist seem like a good investment?

10875 Main Street ~ Suite 205 ▪ Fairfax, VA 22030 USA ▪ 703-359-6000

www.MktgSols.com ▪ MktgSols@MktgSols.com ▪ Fax: 703-934-5490

Renaissance Salons & Day Spas

Sunday, January 30, 2005 ~ Photography Session

WARDROBE CHECKLIST:

MODEL'S NAME: ______________________ MODEL CALL TIME: 8:00 AM

WOMEN ~ Bring 5 to 8 Outfits:

- ❑ **3 to 4 Fancy Dress Blouses** — **Interesting colors, necklines and daring shapes**; Anything dramatic or unusual
- ❑ **2 Fancy Work or 'Cocktail' Dresses** — Or Pant Suits. This Includes strapless, spaghetti strap or cocktail dresses; **Please advise us if you have the availability of a 'Wedding Dress'**
- ❑ **1 Blazer or Suit** — Dressy Career or Casual Styles
- ❑ **1 Black Dress Slacks or Skirt** — Solid black
- ❑ **1 Leather & / Or 1 Jeans Jacket** — Solid colors - The more creative -- the better!
- ❑ **Assorted Accessories** — **Scarves, ties, sunglasses, gloves, hats, props**
- ❑ **Strapless Bra and & or a Tube Top** — Plain, no patterns. Include a black or nude color bra, if possible
- ❑ **Assorted 'Very Simple' Jewelry** — Earring studs - diamond, pearl, gold, silver, black or white; Simple necklaces and any available avant garde / costume jewelry; AVOID large 'dangle' earrings or ornate jewelry! Jewelry must be limited
- ❑ Makeup — **IMPORTANT!!! - COME WITH 'NO MAKEUP' ON**; Bring your own favorite skincare and makeup - as possible 'extras'
- ❑ Nails — **Must have nails clean, filed and polished***

MEN ~ Bring 4 to 5 Outfits:

- ❑ **3 to 4 Dress Shirts** — Oxfords, button downs, tuxedo style, etc. - ***IRONED***
- ❑ 2 Casual Shirts — With collars
- ❑ **2 Sport Coats or Blazers** — A suit or an extra - 'Tuxedo Look' is fine
- ❑ **1 Pair Black Dress Slacks** — Solid black
- ❑ **1 Vest** - If available — Casual or dressy
- ❑ 1 or 2 Assorted Colored T-Shirts — And / or muscle shirts - solid colors / no logos
- ❑ **A Few Assorted Accessories** / Props — Examples: Ties, sunglasses, bow ties, suspenders or gloves
- ❑ 1 Leather or 1 Jeans Jacket — Solid colors - No decorations or patterns
- ❑ Razor & Shaving Cream — Come 'clean-shaved', unless otherwise directed - or bring kit
- ❑ Nails — Must have nails clean and filed*

*** We will have hairstylists, aestheticians, makeup and nailcare artists ready to perform all of your services!**

IMPORTANT: **Please bring all wardrobe clean, ironed and on hangers!** We must assume no responsibility for any loss or damage of wardrobe at shoot. We do ask that you help us carefully watch your personal wardrobe for its safe use during this photo session.

SOLID COLORS ARE THE BEST!!! . . . **WEAR: Black, Brown, Cream, Tan, Blue, Red, Burgundy, Gold, Silver or Grey**
. . . **WHITE & Off-White wardrobe pieces are fine, yet will be used mostly as accents**

AVOID - most prints, big patterns, polka dots, plaids and stripes on entire wardrobe selection
AVOID - bright green and orange clothing selections
AVOID - seasonality in clothing choices, unless otherwise specified

HAIR: Come with hair as is!!! - NOT pre-styled or pre-cut! Just clean & shampooed, unless otherwise instructed. Haircutting and hairstyling will take place at photo-session after a necessary 'before photo' is taken.

QUESTIONS? Call Sharon, Kim,Jennifer or Melissa at Renaissance Salon & Day Spa in Frederick, MD: 301-682-3313
Or -- At their Hunt Valley Location: 410-527-1175, their Bel-Air Location: 410-893-4247
Or -- Call Ashleigh Irving or Larry Oskin at Marketing Solutions in Fairfax, VA ~ 703-359-6000

Notes

Notes

TARGETING PUBLICATIONS

A comprehensive plan to succeed requires a goal. Targeting means identifying which publications are likely to accept your work. Start the process by learning what specialty hair magazines are on the market and the type of photos they typically publish. You probably already know many of the hair magazines, including some in which your styles would look right at home. The idea is to identify and find several similar magazines because your photo shoot is going to be expensive and you'll want to get as much mileage from it as possible. The more magazines you send photos to, the better your chances of getting something accepted.

Study the magazines you have in the salon. Check the newsstands, big chain bookstores and supermarkets for additional ones. And, of course, get on the Internet. It offers information about more magazines than local stores can carry. Many magazines have Web sites and even more will in the future. You'll see the kind of hairstyles they publish, as well as the fashions that accompany them.

If this research seems daunting, don't despair. Below you'll find a list of the most important magazines and publishing groups in the hair industry, along with contact information. Purchase a sample copy of a few magazines that you're unfamiliar with.

Hair magazines run the gamut from utilitarian collections of mainstream styles to very slick productions with an eye to high fashion. They all have definable audiences and uses, and are distributed through different channels. But basically, they fall into four main categories:

1. Many of the hair magazines are sold on newsstands and reach a large mainstream audience. Don't overlook these **consumer publications**. They might be inexpensive, but they sell really well.

Black Hairstyles & Trends
Black Hair & Braids
Bridal Star Hairstyles
Celebrity Cuts Hairstyles & Trends
Celebrity Hairstyles
Celebrity 101 Hairstyles
Celebrity Shortcuts
Celebrity Style 101 Salon Select

Cutting Edge
Hairdo Ideas
Hype Hair
New Ideas for Hairstyling
Seventeen Hair
Short Hairstyles
Short & Easy Hairstyles
Short & Sexy Hairstyles
Sophisticate's Black Hair
Sophisticate's Hairstyle Guide
Step-by-Step Hairstyling
The Complete Hairstyle Guide
Today's Hair
Total Image

2. **Salon selectors** provide ideas for clients waiting to be styled. And stylists often use them to explain what they're about to create.

Black Passion
Coiffure-Q
Color of Passion
Gran'Chic
Inspire
Men's Passion
Passion
Upstyles & Weddings

3. Upscale salons in major cities always have **artists' books** in the waiting area. Their styles tend to be avant-garde.

Elite
Studio
Nobu

4. Magazines devoted to **salon management** also run hair photos.

American Salon
Day Spa
Estetica
Modern Salon
Process
Salon Today
Salón Plus

Notes

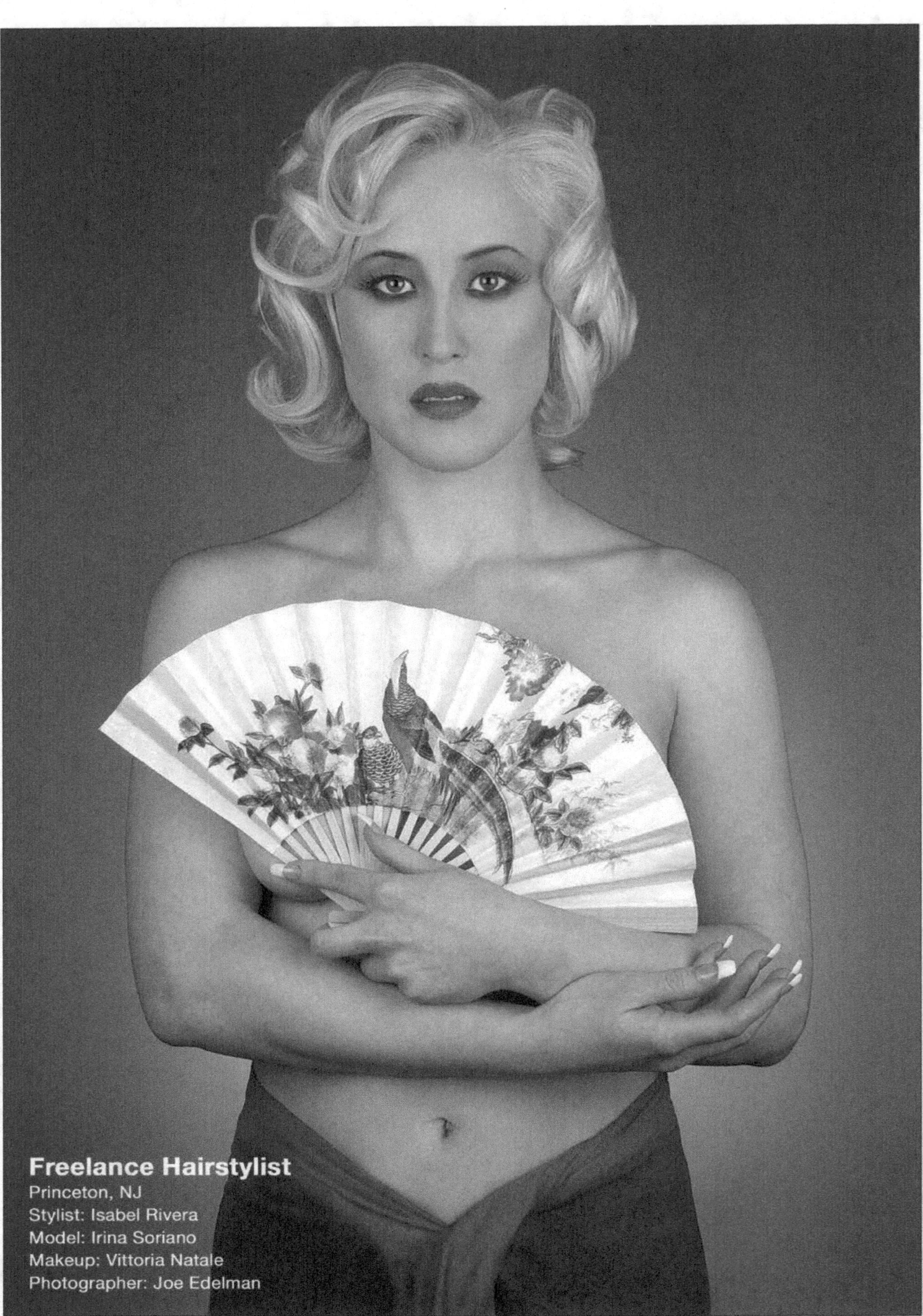
Freelance Hairstylist
Princeton, NJ
Stylist: Isabel Rivera
Model: Irina Soriano
Makeup: Vittoria Natale
Photographer: Joe Edelman

Regina Webb Salon & Spa
Passion Partners: Bowling Green, KY
Stylist: Regina Webb
Colorist: Regina Webb
Model: Dierdra
Makeup: Vittoria Natale
Photographer: Tom Carson

Regina Webb Salon & Spa
Passion Partners: Bowling Green, KY
Stylist: Regina Webb
Colorist: Regina Webb
Model: Jaclyn
Makeup: Vittoria Natale
Photographer: Tom Carson

Regina Webb Salon & Spa
Passion Partners: Bowling Green, KY
Stylist: Regina Webb
Colorist: Regina Webb
Model: Dierdra
Makeup: Vittoria Natale
Photographer: Tom Carson

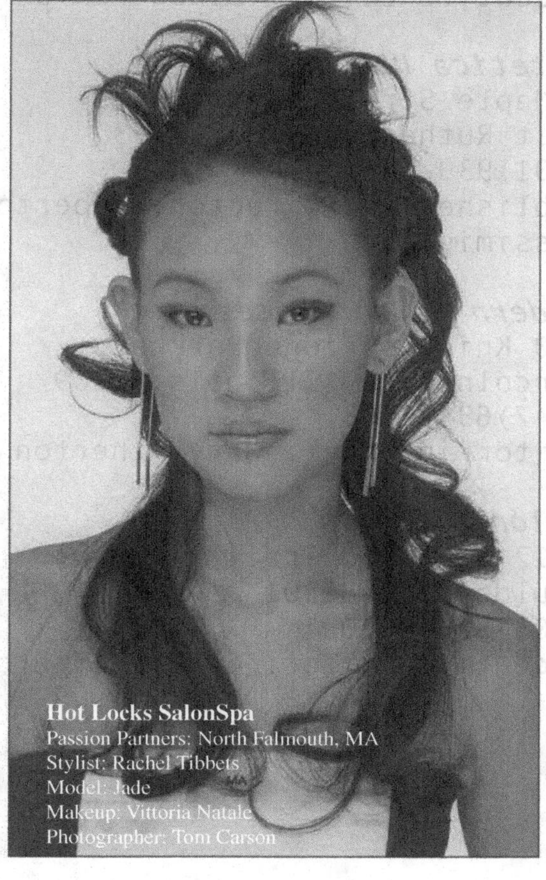

Hot Locks SalonSpa
Passion Partners: North Falmouth, MA
Stylist: Rachel Tibbets
Model: Jade
Makeup: Vittoria Natale
Photographer: Tom Carson

MANAGEMENT PUBLICATIONS CONTACT INFORMATION

The contact person for each magazine could change. Call to verify the name before mailing anything to the magazine.

American Salon-East Coast
One Park Avenue
NY, NY 10016
(212)951-6600
Editor-in-Chief: Robbin McClain

American Salon-West Coast
827 Cypress Ct.
Thousand Oaks, CA 91320
Editor-in-Chief: Kelly Donahu
(805)376-9592

Day Spa Magazine
7628 Densmore Avenue
Van Nuys, CA 91406
(818)782-7328
Executive Editor: Linda Lewis

Estetica USA New York
1 Maple Street, Unit 8A
East Rutherford, NJ 07073
(201)939-1411
Publisher and Director: Roberto Pissimiglia

Modern Salon/Process
400 Knightsbridge Parkway
Lincolnshire, Illinois 60069
(847)634-2600
Editor-in-Chief: Mary Atherton

Salón Plus
5412 Idylwild Trail
Boulder, CO 80301
(303)516-9690
Executive Editor: Carla Vottero

Salon Today
400 Knightsbridge Parkway
Lincolnshire, Illinois 60059
(847)634-2600
Editor-in-Chief: Laurel Smoke

CONSUMER/NEWSSTAND PUBLICATIONS CONTACT INFORMATION

The contact person for each magazine could change. Call to verify the name before mailing anything to the magazine.

Bridal Star Hairstyles
Celebrity Hairstyles
Hairdo Ideas
New Ideas for Hairstyling
Short Hair
The Complete Hairstyle Guide
Harris Publications, Inc.
1115 Broadway
NY, NY 10010
(212)807-7100
Editor: Mary Greenberg
(A stamped, self-addressed envelope must accompany submissions and/or photographs).

Celebrity Shortcuts
Celebrity 101 Hairstyles
Celebrity Style 101
Salon Select
Multi-media International, LLC
1359 Broadway, Suite 1203
NY, NY 10018
(212)244-0559
Editor-in-Chief: Cheryl Schwartz

Hype Hair
Mitchell Advertising Group
201 Route 4 East
Suite 211
Paramus, NJ 07652
(201)843-4004 ext. 130
Editor-in-Chief: Adrienne Moore

Sophisticate's Black Hair
Sophisticate's Hairstyle Guide
Associated Publications, Inc.
John Hancock Center
875 North Michigan Avenue
Suite 3434

Chicago, Illinois 60611
(312)266-8680
Editor-in-Chief: Bonnie Krueger

Short & Sexy Hairstyles
Step-by-Step Hairstyling
Short Hairstyles*
(Send all photos, slides or CD's to: ***Short Hairstyles*** attn: Sandy Kosherick)
Goodman Media Group, Inc.
250 West 57th Street
Suite 710
NY, NY 10107
(212)262-2247
Editor-in-Chief: Shelly-Dawson Davies
Important**: Every single slide, transparency or photograph must be labeled with the stylist's name, salon or company name, photographer, makeup artist and any other information you'd like to include. ***Short Hairstyles will not use art that is not labeled.

Short & Easy Hairstyles
Roxbury Media, LLC
27 Glenn Road
P.O. Box 140
Sandy Hook, CT 06482
(203)270-8572
Editor-in-Chief: Stephanie Pedersen
Editorial Offices for Roxbury Media
P.O. Box 165
Englishtown, NJ 07726
(732)786-8044
Editor: Dorothy Creamer

Seventeen Hair
Hearst Communications, Inc.
NY, NY
(212)204-4300 New York Office
(312)396-0613 Chicago Office
Bookings Editor: Jennifer Baptista
Shootings Coordinator: Erica Saiger
Editor-in-Chief: Sabrina Weill

Total Image
C&C Media, LLC
2108 South Blvd.

Vittoria Natale
Suite 102
Charlotte, NC 28203
(704)287-1006
totalimagemag@aol.com
Editor-in-Chief: Nina Laroux
Publisher: Tom Carson

Notes

SALON SELECTORS
CONTACT INFORMATION

The contact person for each magazine could change. Call to verify the name before mailing anything to the magazine.

Black Passion
Color of Passion
Upstyles & Weddings
Passion Beauty, Inc.
11953 South Prairie Avenue
Los Angeles, CA 90250
(800)362-7071
Publisher: Dan Funk
www.passionbeauty.com

Coiffure-Q
Men's Passion
Passion
Dowa International
Unit 8 Hanover West Industrial Estate
160 Action Lane
London, England NW107NB

Elite
Pulse Longcroft Windmill Park
Wroth Heath Kent TN 157SY UK
(441)732-88-2181
USA, Jim Cohen
EEC, Frank Dickman
Editor, Beverly Cupon

Gran'Chic
Via A. Saffi 11
20123 Milano, Italy
Editor, Mr. Trinchinetti
www.granchic.com

Inspire
Creative Age Publications
7628 Densmore Avenue
Van Nuys, CA 91406
(818)782-7328 or (800)442-5667
Editor: Cheryl Lenskes
www.inspirequarterly.co

Notes

Notes

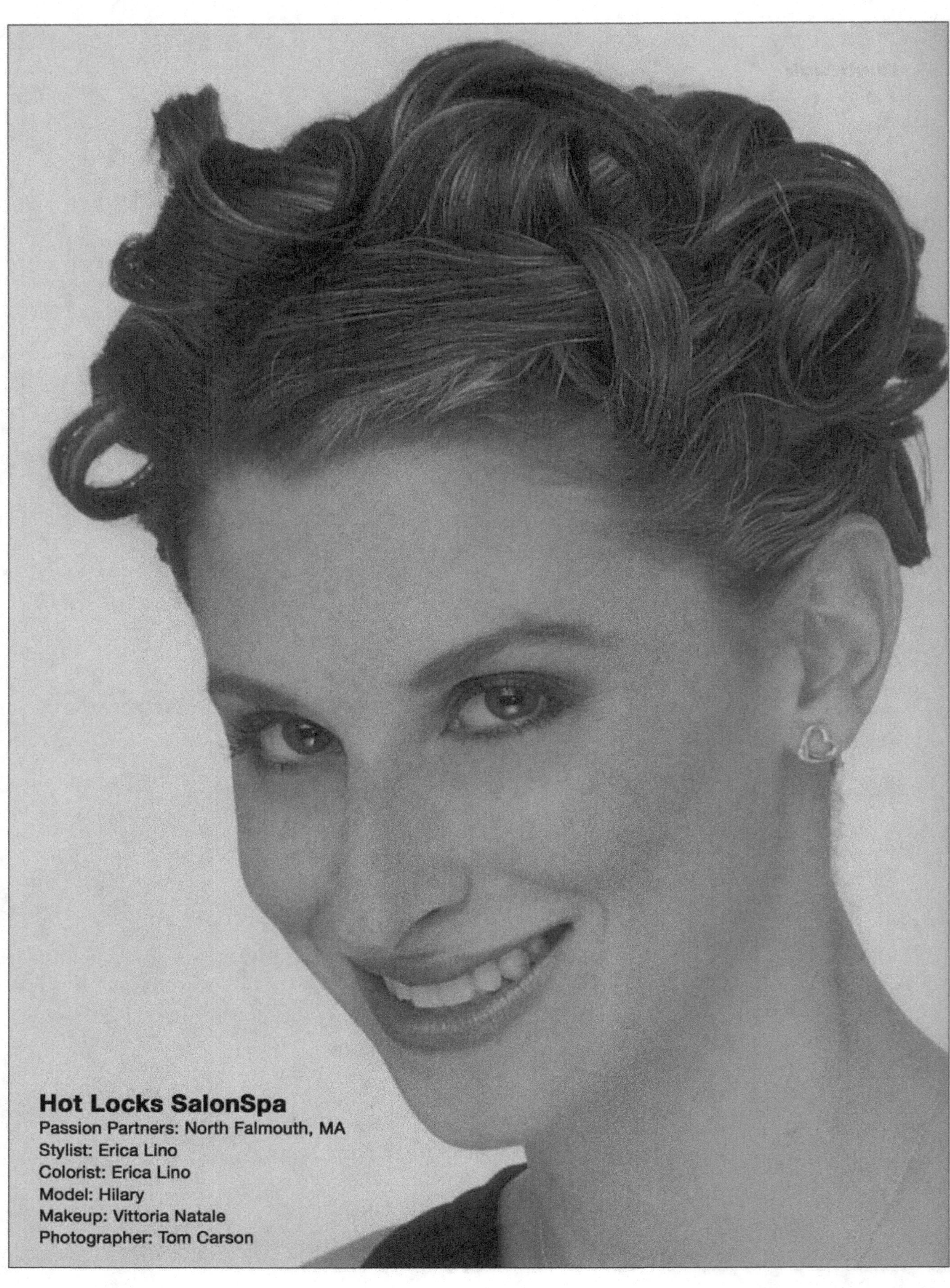

Hot Locks SalonSpa
Passion Partners: North Falmouth, MA
Stylist: Erica Lino
Colorist: Erica Lino
Model: Hilary
Makeup: Vittoria Natale
Photographer: Tom Carson

Hot Locks SalonSpa
Passion Partners: North Falmouth, MA
Stylist: Stephanie Lawson
Colorist: Stephanie Lawson
Model: Gina
Makeup: Vittoria Natale
Photographer: Tom Carson

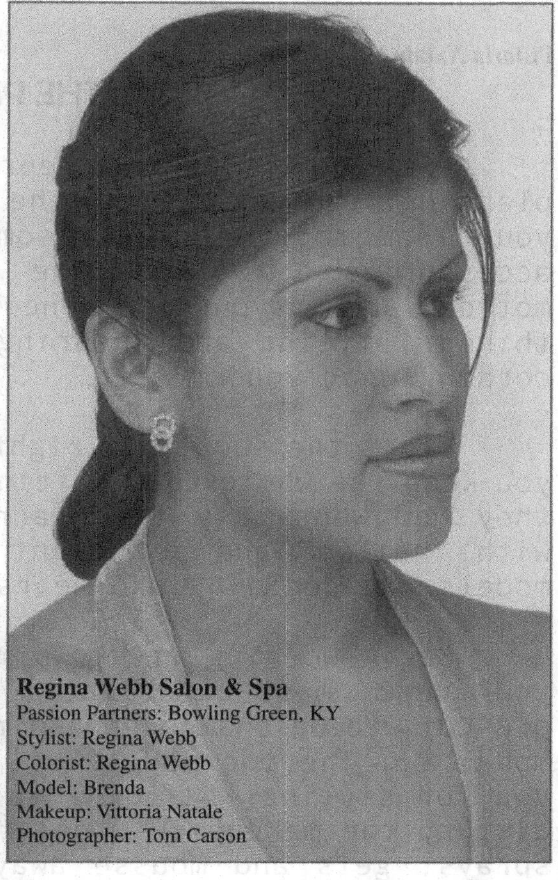

Regina Webb Salon & Spa
Passion Partners: Bowling Green, KY
Stylist: Regina Webb
Colorist: Regina Webb
Model: Brenda
Makeup: Vittoria Natale
Photographer: Tom Carson

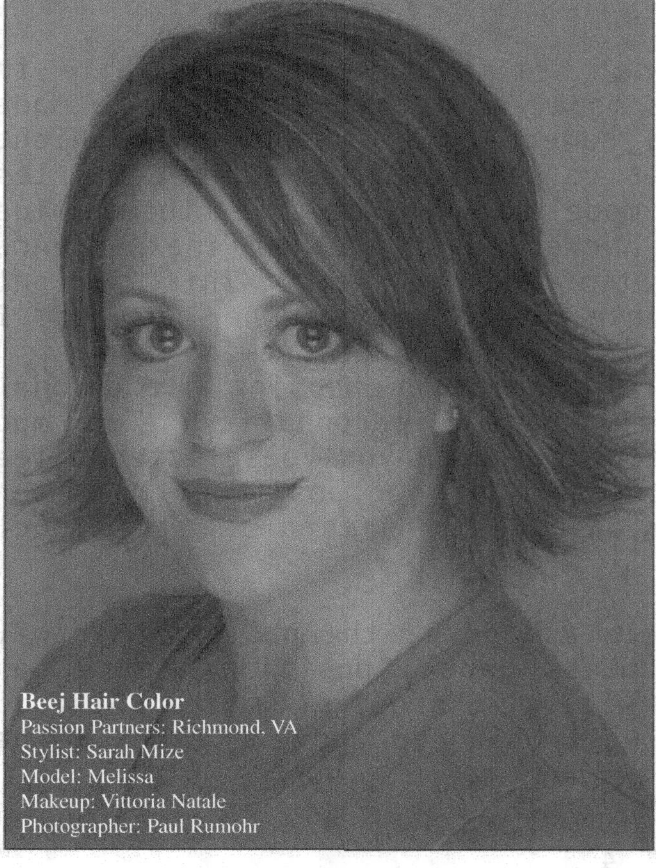

Beej Hair Color
Passion Partners: Richmond. VA
Stylist: Sarah Mize
Model: Melissa
Makeup: Vittoria Natale
Photographer: Paul Rumohr

Salon Gallimore
Passion Partners: Cherry Hill, NJ
Stylist: Christine McClure
Model: Maria Gingrich, Bowman Agency
Makeup: Vittoria Natale
Photographer: Gary Mattie

THE PHOTO SESSION

The photo session represents the culmination of lots of planning: You've selected the looks you're going to create, brought your team together, done some pre-cuts, and assembled fashions, accessories and props. The time has come to set everything in motion. And if you've planned well, you'll be able to focus on two things: styling and insuring that the camera is faithfully recording what you created.

Start the shoot off right by getting to the studio on time. If you keep the whole team waiting, they'll never recover the momentum they had when they first arrived. Dispense quickly and politely with "hellos" and get right to work, establishing the order of models and deciding who wears what.

Begin working with two models simultaneously. They should be your best, most experienced models. Send model #1, who has been pre-cut, to be shampooed and made-up. Shampoo and style the hair of model #2. The two models will then switch stations, #1 coming to you for styling, #2 going to the makeup artist. Take care not to disturb the makeup on model #1 while you style her hair, and keep sprays, gels and mousse away from her face because they create shiny areas on the skin.

Never make your lead model sit around and wait while the others are prepped. As soon as model #1 or #2 is styled and made-up, she should go before the camera. The first model finished (either #1 or #2) is the first to be photographed. Let the less experienced models watch these models work. This gives them an idea of what you expect from them. Never, ever, let an inexperienced model go first and have the rest of the crew watch. This will only draw attention to her lack of experience and make her nervous. If you haven't worked with any of the models before—and none is a professional model—go with your instincts in choosing a lead model. Don't be fooled by an overly bubbly personality. Too much enthusiasm may be masking insecurity. Once you've selected a lead model, explain to her the importance of her position. Make sure your assistant also knows in advance in what order the models should go.

While you're styling models #1 and 2, the photographer will set up the background of seamless paper, position lights, and take meter readings. He or she will also shoot off a few Polaroids to make sure the lighting is well-balanced and the exposure has been properly calculated. When the lighting is finalized, make whatever adjustments are necessary to the model's hair. And show the photographer what aspect of the hairstyle you want emphasized.

You're ready now for the first image. Most photographers will shoot an initial Polaroid to allow everyone to examine the shot before putting it on film. The image will be slightly different from what your eye sees, because the camera's sight line is different from that of a bystander. It also picks up defects that the eye ignores. Using a loupe to magnify the image, study the Polaroid carefully. Check the hair. Is everything in place? Are there any holes where light shows through. Make adjustments, but don't overwork the hair.

Polaroids don't have the tonal range of regular film and won't render color faithfully, but they will provide a good sense of how the image fills the frame, how the hair and makeup look and whether or not the lighting is advantageous. If the photographer is shooting with a digital camera, you'll be able to examine the image on the camera's external screen. Whatever the format, it's worth paying attention to these test shots.

When all adjustments are made, the photographer will start shooting. He or she is in charge now and will give directions to the model. A rhythm will be established between the two that no one must break. If you have something to say—suppose you spot a flaw in the hair—direct your comments to the photographer. A professional model is trained to respond only to the photographer and will not stop working at your bidding.

This is an aspect of studio etiquette, one that recognizes that in this environment the photographer is boss. And even though the day's activity is coming out of your pocket, you're really only a guest in the photographer's house. There are a few other like-minded studio tips worth knowing:

Never walk on the paper covering the floor where the model is posing. Your shoes will dirty it, making it unusable.

Never walk on the set without permission. And if you're asked to adjust the model's hair on the set, take off your shoes before you do it.

Never touch or move a light. You can screw up the photographer's carefully calculated exposure.

Never stand in front of or to the side of a light. It's easy to block light without realizing what you're doing. It's also easy to kick one of the splayed legs of a light stand, moving the light or overturning it. It's best to stand three or four feet directly behind the camera, where you won't interfere with the photographer's movements and where you'll get a good approximation of what the camera is seeing.

When three styles have been photographed, it'll be time to break for lunch. Arranging for and setting out food are tasks that you might assign to your assistant. Assorted salads, cold cuts and fruit make for a nice light lunch. Be sure to include vegetarian selections, as well as plenty of different drinks. Non-alcoholic of course. Aside from the obvious fact that you want everyone at full mental capacity, you don't want to expose yourself to a possible lawsuit, should there be an accident. Leave the food out for the rest of the day in case anyone needs a snack.

After lunch, you'll continue preparing and photographing additional looks. These can be more intense than those done in the morning. Because, it's easier for the makeup artist, for example, to apply a heavier, more dramatic look over a soft, light, daytime design than the reverse application. The set, lighting and fashions can equally be heightened.

After the shoot is complete, but before anyone leaves, pay the models and anyone else you've agreed to pay. Make sure every model signs a release form. The pictures can't be used without one. It will be a long day but an exciting one. You should be able to photograph six to eight looks.

Notes

Regina Webb Salon & Spa
Passion Partners: Bowling Green, KY
Stylist: Regina Webb
Model: Dawne
Makeup: Vittoria Natale
Photographer: Paul Rumohr

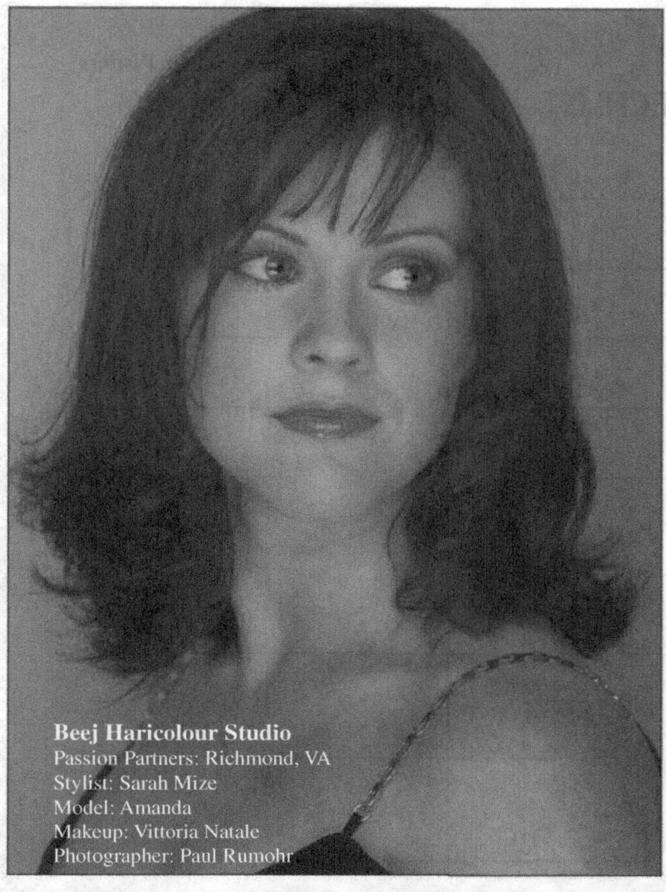

Beej Haricolour Studio
Passion Partners: Richmond, VA
Stylist: Sarah Mize
Model: Amanda
Makeup: Vittoria Natale
Photographer: Paul Rumohr

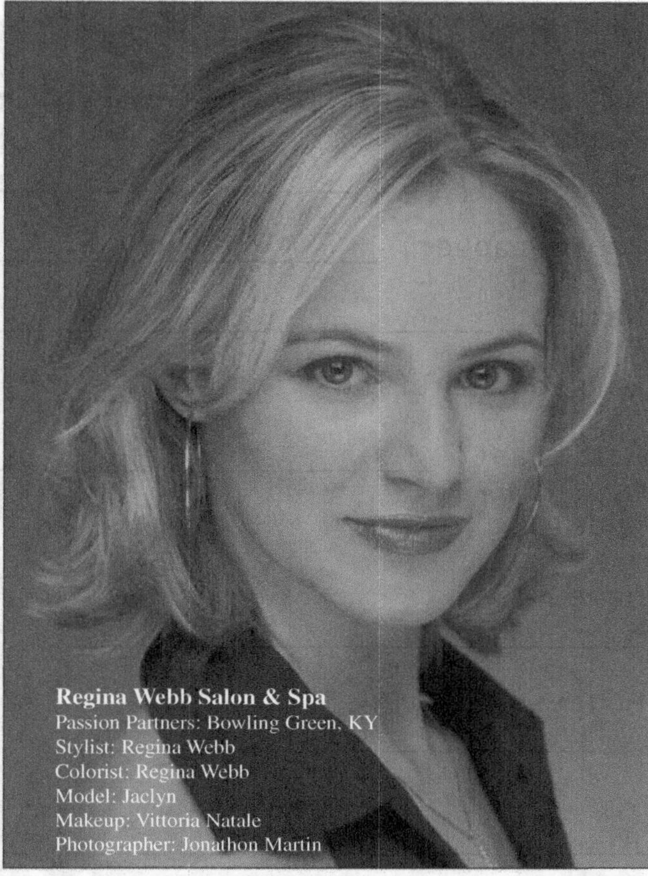

Regina Webb Salon & Spa
Passion Partners: Bowling Green, KY
Stylist: Regina Webb
Colorist: Regina Webb
Model: Jaclyn
Makeup: Vittoria Natale
Photographer: Jonathon Martin

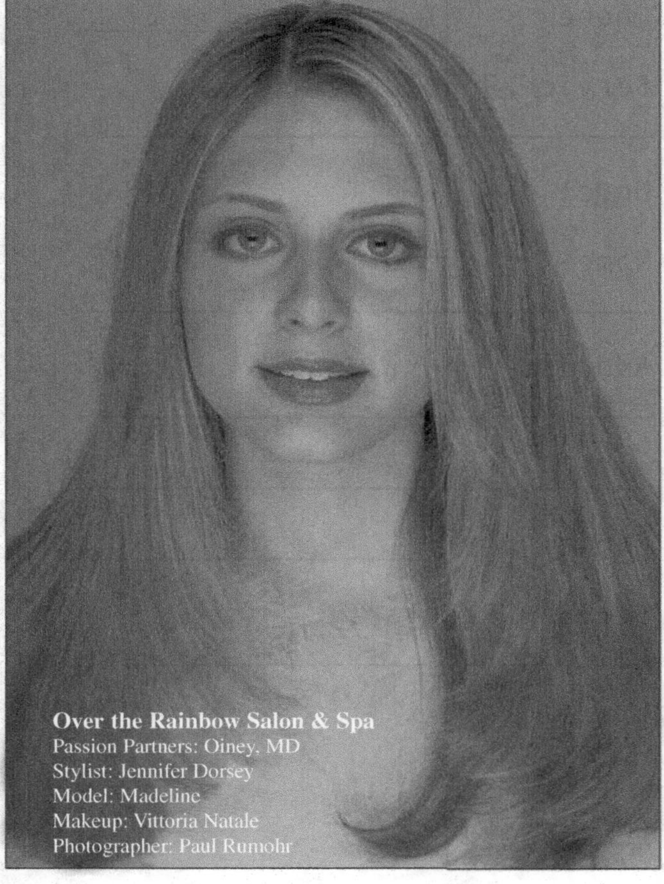

Over the Rainbow Salon & Spa
Passion Partners: Oiney, MD
Stylist: Jennifer Dorsey
Model: Madeline
Makeup: Vittoria Natale
Photographer: Paul Rumohr

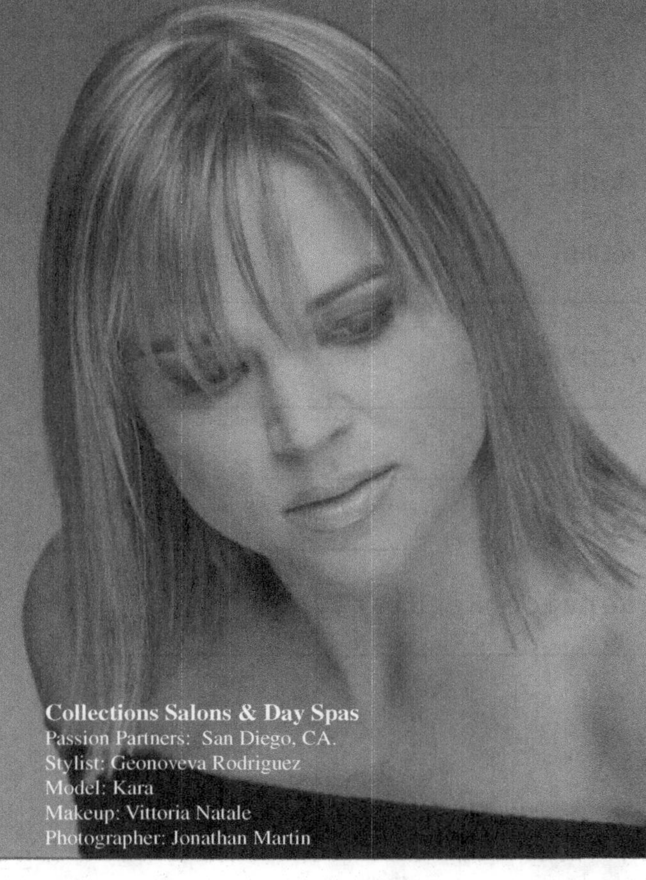

Collections Salons & Day Spas
Passion Partners: San Diego, CA.
Stylist: Geonoveva Rodriguez
Model: Kara
Makeup: Vittoria Natale
Photographer: Jonathan Martin

SESSION CHECKLIST

Starting Time: ______________________________

Photographer: ______________________________ Phone: (   )__________

Makeup: ______________________________ Phone: (   )__________

Fashion Stylist: ______________________________ Phone: (   )__________

Assistant: ______________________________ Phone: (   )__________

Model 1

Name

____

Address

____

____

Phone (   )__________________

Service Regularly

____

Model 2

Name

____

Address

____

____

Phone (   )__________________

Service Regularly

____

Model 3

Name

____

Address

____

____

Phone (   )__________________

Service Regularly

____

Model 4

Name

____

Address

____

____

Phone (   )__________________

Service Regularly

____

Notes

RELEASE FORM

NAME:______________________________ ADDRESS:______________________________

____

____

DATE:______________________________ PHONE#: ______________________________

I hereby give____________________, photographer, and/or __________________________ stylist, the absolute right and permission to copyright and/or publish, or use photographic portraits or pictures of me, in which I may be included in whole or part, composite, in conjunction with my own or a fictitious name, or reproductions thereof in color or otherwise, made through media at the studio or elsewhere, for art, advertising, trade, or any other lawful purpose whatsoever.

I hereby waive any rights that I have to inspect and/or approve the finished product or the advertising copy or printed matter that may be used in connection therewith, or use to which it may be applied.

I hereby release, discharge, and agree to save the photographer and the stylist from any liability by virtue of blurring, distortion, alteration, optical illusion, or use in composite form whether intentional or otherwise, that may occur or be produced in the completion of the finished product, or its publication or distribution.

☐ I hereby represent that I am over the age of 18 years and I have read this authorization and release prior to its execution.

☐ I am under 18 and have the consent of my parents or guardian.

______________________________ ______________________________
MODEL/PARENT OR GUARDIAN WITNESS

______________________________ ______________________________
PHOTOGRAPHER HAIRSTYLIST

For all reproduction rights to the above-mentioned photographs photographed on this date and/or editorial material in any issue of any Hair or Beauty trade publication and/or promotional material.

Notes

EDITING

Within a matter of days after the shoot, you should receive contact sheets of the black-and-white images and slides of the color ones. The contact sheet contains little pictures of the same size as the film, which means they're often too small to evaluate properly without a magnifying glass or loupe. Sit beside a light when using a loupe, taking care to keep your fingers off the side closest to the light. The slides (also called transparencies) are equally small and should be projected on a screen or blank wall. All flaws are readily apparent when the image is enlarged to something like 20 by 30 inches. You can also check out slides by placing them on a light box and viewing them through a loupe.

It's now time to take an objective look at the images. Forget about who looks best off-camera. Forget about how nice this one was to model for free. And especially forget about how much that one would love to appear in a magazine. The only important consideration is, which images best illustrate your styling ***and*** the model's great face? Eliminate frames that have imperfections, such as closed eyes, confusing shadows, weak expressions, misplaced hair and creased clothing. The list of mistakes can grow infuriatingly long. Hopefully you'll find five to ten great frames of each style.

You should review the black-and-white images first in order to give the photographer enough time to make prints. Working right on the contact sheet, mark the images you like with a grease pencil. This is better than making a list of the frames you want printed, because there's no chance of misreading or misprinting the frame number, which is inconspicuously printed on the horizontal border of the film. You can ask the photographer to make proofs—these are trial prints, not final ones—of the selected frames. Or based on your reading of the contact sheet, you can request finished prints. Indicate how many copies of each print you want.

Review the color slides with similar care. On a first run-through, eliminate all that have obvious problems. On a second round, sort the slides according to the publications you've targeted and put them into plastic pages, using a separate page for each magazine. Write the name of the magazine at the top of each page.

You lose quality when you duplicate slides, so always send originals. If your photographer shoots lots of transparencies, you'll have the material you need. It's important to mention at the time of the photo shoot that you'd like to send out several versions of the hairstyle and therefore want lots of different angles.

Follow the same selection procedures with digital images. The only difference is where you edit the photographs. You will receive a CD or a contact sheet with all of the images on it. The images will be viewed on a computer or on contact sheets through a loupe versus a slide projector. Make a list of which pictures you want to keep and where you want to send them. After you've finished making selections, review your choices with the photographer so he or she can copy the photos onto a separate CD for each magazine. During the review and selection process, you can also direct the photographer how to crop a photo or adjust its color. You can also indicate places that need retouching. Label each CD with the magazine's name and credit information before sending it to the publication.

Notes

The Final Stage

It's almost time to package your work for mailing. But first you have to write captions for the chosen looks and also identify the creative team on every print and slide.

Write a short paragraph that describes each of the styles you're sending. Hold the jargon and keep your language simple. But describe the cut with the assurance of the expert that you are. For example: "This striking blunt bob with an elevated back and soft wispy bangs is bold and futuristic. Add dramatic forward motion to the hair and you're definitely in style." Number the looks and place the corresponding number on the descriptive paragraph.

Finally, label each print and slide with the salon name, your name, haircolorist, makeup artist, photographer, fashion stylist and model. Use this shorthand because writing space is limited:
Salon:
Hair:
HairColor:(if different from hairstylist)
Makeup:
Photo:
Fashion:
Model:

When working with a fashion stylist, also provide the names of the clothing designer and the retailer who lent the merchandise. If you used a professional model, supply the name of his or her agency. If you can't fit all of this information on a slide, or if it's difficult to read on the slide, prepare a separate sheet using the same numbering system you created with captions.

Include postage with the photos and slides so that the magazines will mail the work back in case they can't use it. This will allow you to send the images to another magazine. If a magazine uses images, they pay to send them back. The images are the property of the stylist whether the magazine uses them or not. Images should always be returned.

Notes

INTERNATIONAL SUBMISSIONS

Sending a submission overseas should be no more difficult than sending a package next door. However, if you don't supply the right paperwork, your mailing can be held up in customs and you might miss a magazine's deadline.

International shipments require a customs declaration and/or a commercial invoice. Since you'll be sending editorial material, the customs declaration is quite simple. (See form on page 54)

When you fill out the form, write $10 under both "value" and "value for carriage." Since the carrier is only responsible for replacement costs, there's no need to incur higher charges for greater protection. Replacement costs here mean the cost of film and processing, and not the big bucks you paid to have the images created. You can and should insure the contents of the package to cover your actual costs.

Federal Express (FedEx) is the most reliable shipper. It requires the recipient's signature, tracks packages efficiently and provides itemized bills. And when your package arrives in a foreign country, Federal Express's own couriers deliver it. All the forms required for an international mailing are also on its Web site.

Notes

CUSTOMS DECLARATION

Receiving Party

To: ______________________

Attn: ______________________

____

____

____

I understand and do hereby declare the following contents to be true and correct.

Quantity	Description	Country of Origin
________	Color Transparencies	USA
________	Black & White Photos	USA
________	Color Photos	USA
________	CDs	USA

The above material has ______________ commercial value.

Value for carriage ________________.

Sending Party

Name ______________________ Phone ( ) __________

Address ____

City ______________________ State ______ Zip ______

Country ____________________

Notes

FOLLOW-UP

Follow-up occurs on two fronts: with the magazines where you've submitted work and at home in your files.

It's okay to confirm with a magazine that your mailing has arrived. It's also okay to check on the status of your submission if a month goes by and you don't hear from the editor. Most editors will notify you promptly once they make a decision. They know very quickly when they love or hate something. They keep you dangling when they're uncertain about the photos ("great" but we have no use for them right now or "so-so" but they could come in handy if they don't have enough submissions). Don't make repeated calls. You'll quickly be named "the pest," and they won't want to do business with you then or later.

However, you shouldn't leave your work at any magazine indefinitely. Remember that the images belong to you and should be returned to you. If the magazine rejects your work, they should return it, using the stamps you enclosed with your submission.

Whether your work is accepted or rejected, it's good form to write a brief, business-style note that says, "thanks for publishing (or considering) my work." Your goal is to develop a working relationship with the editor. Once you've accomplished this, you can phone to say thanks and inquire at the same time if they might assign you to do something special.

Never question editors' decisions not to use your work. They know best what will work in their publications. Unfortunately, they usually don't have or take the time to explain why your images don't fit their concept of their magazine. You'll learn soon enough, however, what a particular magazine wants by keeping good records of what gets accepted.

Create a manila folder for each photo shoot. In it keep a tracking sheet with the following information: date of photo session, photographer, makeup artist, fashion stylist, assistant, models. The folder should also include numbered Polaroids of the hairstyles and signed model releases. Each time one of your styles is published, list the publication, the issue in which it was published and the number of the look that was accepted. Number the folder by giving it the date of the photo shoot (2005,January 9 becomes 050109). The folders should be placed in descending numerical order so that your most current work will always be in front.

When a magazine accepts your work and you make entries on the tracking sheet, spend some time reviewing the Polaroids. You'll soon know which styles work with which magazines and also which models are bringing you the most success.

Notes

TRACKING SHEET

Session Day: ____________ Date: ____________ Year: ____________

Photographer: ____________________ Phone: ( ) ________________

Assistant: ________________________ Phone: ( ) ________________

Makeup: __________________________ Phone: ( ) ________________

Fashion: _________________________ Phone: ( ) ________________

Model 1: _________________________ Phone: ( ) ________________

Model 2: _________________________ Phone: ( ) ________________

Model 3: _________________________ Phone: ( ) ________________

Model 4: _________________________ Phone: ( ) ________________

Date Submitted: __________________

Date Notified: ___________________ Accepted/Rejected: ____________

	Publication	Issue	Style#
1.	____________________	______	______
2.	____________________	______	______
3.	____________________	______	______
4.	____________________	______	______
5.	____________________	______	______
6.	____________________	______	______
7.	____________________	______	______
8.	____________________	______	______
9.	____________________	______	______

Notes

PHOTOGRAPHERS

A full-service photographer is good for a hairstylist who just wants to do hair and prefers not to have to deal with submissions, selecting a team etc. The stylist can rely on the expertise of the photographer or a marketing company for this handoff of services and pay a premium. Several of the recommended photographers are full-service photographers. All of them are well-known and have been published in beauty trade magazines.

Eric Von Lockart
Studio I NYC Inc./Full Service
231 West 29th Street
Suite 901
New York, NY 10001
(212)268-4088
www.ericvonlockart.com

Gary Mattie
Mattie Studio, Inc.
1008 Astoria Boulevard
Suite G
Cherry Hill, NJ 08003
(856)874-0404
(888)222-7950
www.mattiestudio.com

Joe Chielli
Church Street Studios
122 Church Street
Philadelphia, PA 19106
(215)627-2420
www.churchstreetstudios.com

Joe Edelman PhotographicS
P.O. Box 962
Landsdale, PA 19446
(215)412-7004
www.JoeEdelman.com

Paul Rumohr
Paul Rumohr Photography
410 West Milford Street
Suite 201
Glendale, CA 91203
(213)400-8006
www.paulrumohr.com

Purely Visual Productions/Full Service
Kelly Taggart
David Winterhalter
8502 East Chapman Avenue
Suite 610
Orange Hills, CA 92869
(714)532-4772

Rudi Weislein Photography
5740 West Centinela Avenue
Suite 222
Los Angeles, CA 90045
(310)342-0091
www.weislein.com

Tom Carson Photography/Full Service
2108 South Boulevard
Suite 102
Charlotte, NC 28203
(704)364-6457
E-Mail:CarsonPhoto@aol.com

Alexi Afonin
Alexei Productions
396 Broadway
Suite 800
New York, NY 10013
(212)966-9290
www.alexeipro.com

Chip Foust
114 Sunset Boulevard
Asheboro, NC 27203
(336)626-4200
E-Mail: foust@ashboro.com

Jim Arndt
110 North 5th Street
Suite 1135
Minneapolis, MN 55403
(612)332-5050
E-Mail: arndtphoto@aol.com

Jonathan Martin
Magazine Photographic Systems
P.O. Box 6755
Largo, MD 20792-6755
(888)468-5162
E-Mail: jmartin@mps4u.net

Karl Richeson Photography
611 Curtis Avenue
Wilmington, DE 19804
(302)995-1910
www.KarlPhoto.com

Scott Bryant
14709 Hanna Court
Centreville, VA 20101
(571)239-3616
www.scottbryantsbook.com

Another good industry resource:

American Society of Media Photographers
150 North Second Street
Philadelphia, PA 19106
(215)451-ASMP
www.asmp.org

Additional photographers can be found by contacting local Talent and Modeling Agencies.

Notes

MARKETING & PUBLIC RELATIONS OPPORTUNITIES

If you decide to look for a marketing or public relations company to represent you or your salon it is important to find someone that has experience in the beauty business.

Marketing Solutions is one of the very well-known complete marketing, advertising, public relations and consulting service agencies specializing in the professional beauty business. They actively work on a retainer basis with professional salons, day spas, skin care centers, cosmetology academies, plastic surgeons, medical centers, beauty industry manufacturers, distributors, associations and entrepreneurial beauty industry ventures throughout North America. This company schedules nine photography sessions a year in several different locations for ***Passion International Haircolor, Wedding and Family and Upstyles Stylebooks***. The registration fees to participate in each of these photo sessions are $100 to $250 depending on the number of models you present.

Larry Oskin and the Marketing Solutions Team also writes for dozens of national consumer and beauty trade publications. Call or check out their Web site to submit your credentials in order to be considered for one of the 'Top Salons & Day Spas In The USA' Directories.

Contact Information:

Marketing Solutions, Inc.
President, Larry Oskin
Professional Center of Fairfax
10875 Main Street
Suite 205
Fairfax, VA 22030
(703)359-6000
www.MktgSols.com
E-Mail: Loskin@mktgsols.com

Notes

PASSION STYLEBOOK PHOTO SESSIONS
PRESENTED BY MARKETING SOLUTIONS:
CONTACT LARRY OSKIN FOR DATES AND LOCATIONS

Your salon's top hair designers and haircolorists are invited to participate in one of two photography competition sessions for the new Passion Stylebook. This competition stylebook will be devoted to creative haircuts, haircolor, texture and speciality hair designs for women, men and teens. Most models should be between sixteen and forty-five years old. A few children will be accepted. Each participating salon is invited to create special hair designs on three models per registration application.

Models must be VERY attractive and comfortable in front of the camera! All haircutting, haircolor and highlight services must be performed on the models **Before** the day of the shoot, while hairstyles may be finished on location. Makeup, wardrobe, hair ornaments, accessories and finishing touches 'must be provided by you' and can be performed at this photography session.

<u>Registration for available time slots will be taken on a 'FIRST-COME, FIRST-SERVE basis</u> and must be accompanied by a pre-payment of $100. Make registration checks payable to "Marketing Solutions, Inc." for three models. You may submit six models or looks for $175 or nine models and/or total looks for $250. The maximum number of models per salon will be nine. Salons will receive three of the best photographs from their models that get published approximately eight months after the shoot to use for your salon portfolios, advertising, marketing and PR. You will also receive a sample copy of the book!

IMPORTANT: This is a photography competition. Only the very best models, haircolor, hairstyles and makeup will be published.
"Publisher reserves the right to use the model's photographs at their editorial discretion. This is a competition and only the best photographs will be used in the next Passion Haircolor Stylebook.

PASSION PHOTO SESSION & COMPETITION ~ REGISTRATION FORM
PREFERRED START TIMES: Please check one

☐ 8:00 AM ☐ 12:30 PM
☐ 9:00 AM ☐ 2:30 PM
☐ 11:00 AM

Once registered-there will be no refunds for last-minute cancellations.
Your Name: ____________________
Salon Name: ____________________
Salon Address: ____________________
City, State, Zip: ____________________
Salon E-Mail: ____________________
Number of Models: three, six, nine Payment Enclosed $__________

Notes

acknowledgments

First, I would like to thank my extraordinary editor, Gilda Morigi, for her kindness and expertise, I extend to you my unending gratitude and appreciation for your time and for always being there when needed. And a special thank you to Martha Ledger for her choice of words.

To Joe Chielli, a magnificent photographer: It is an honor to have your photos on the cover and inside this publication.

To the special creative photographic talent of Joe Edelman: Thank you for the beautiful photos included in this book.

To Gary Mattie, a unique photographer with extraordinary vision: Thank you for providing the 35mm slide, polaroid and studio shots plus the wonderful, clean, crisp image on the back cover.

A sincere and special thank you to Larry Oskin from Marketing Solutions and to Passion Magazine for supplying the majority of photos that fill this book.

To the many hairstylists, Regina Webb, Regina Webb Salon & Spa, Stephanie Lawson, Erica Lino and Rachel Tibbetts, Hot Locks SalonSpa, Sarah Mize, Beej Haircolor Studio, Genoveva Rodriguez, Collections Salons & Day Spas, Jennifer Dorsey, Over the Rainbow Salon & Spa: Your incredible hair designs will inspire all hairstylists who want to have their work published.

And without the great eyes of the photographers, the photos would not exist. Thank you, Paul Rumohr, Paul Rumohr Photography; Tom Carson, Tom Carson Photography; and Jonathan Martin, Jonathan Martin Photography, for the many beautiful photos.

I would like to pay special thanks to the fantastic models, Alison, Amanda, BriAnna Casantini, Dawne, Deidre, Gina, Hilary, Jaclyn, Jade, Julia Elkouss, Kara, Kiara, Madeline, Melissa and Terry and Maria Gingrich and Megan Wozniak of the Bowman Agency. Mary Bowman, keep dancing always and burn the floor.

To Irina Soriano, a great model: Thank you for allowing us artistic freedom.

To my friend, Denice Monaco: Thank you for your wonderful, creative hairdressing talent.

To Christina McClure and Isabel Rivera: It is always a pleasure to work with great talent.

To James Chielli: Thank you for your amazing creativity in designing the cover.

To Guillermo Elkouss, my love and my inspiration: I want to thank you for your support, devotion, compassion, and generosity. I dedicate this book to you. You mean so much to me. You are a blessing in my life.

I'd also like to acknowledge my mom, Doris; my children, Tammy and Lisa; and my grandchildren, Joseph and BriAnna. I love you all very much.

Notes

Freelance Hairstylist
Princeton, NJ
Stylist: Isabel Rivera
Model: Irina Soriano
Makeup: Vittoria Natale
Photographer: Joe Edelman

Printed in the United States
By Bookmasters